My Worst Boss Ever!

The Unbelievable True Story of a Bigoted Professional and Her Vulgar Ways!

Christopher Lesley

outskirts
press

My Worst Boss Ever!
The Unbelievable True Story of a Bigoted Professional and Her Vulgar Ways!
All Rights Reserved.
Copyright © 2019 Christopher Lesley
v3.0

The opinions expressed in this manuscript are solely the opinions of the author and do not represent the opinions or thoughts of the publisher. The author has represented and warranted full ownership and/or legal right to publish all the materials in this book.

This book may not be reproduced, transmitted, or stored in whole or in part by any means, including graphic, electronic, or mechanical without the express written consent of the publisher except in the case of brief quotations embodied in critical articles and reviews.

Outskirts Press, Inc.
http://www.outskirtspress.com

ISBN: 978-1-9772-1289-4

Cover Photo © 2019 Christopher Lesley.

Outskirts Press and the "OP" logo are trademarks belonging to Outskirts Press, Inc.

PRINTED IN THE UNITED STATES OF AMERICA

Introduction

This is the first writing I've done and it reminded me of one of my favorite Beatles tunes, "Paperback Writer"! It had a calming effect and enabled me to put my bitterness aside to concentrate on telling the actual story. In the process, I gained a profound respect for established authors, and their ability to capture a reader's attention! For me personally, there was a force driving me to document my experience, so I decided to move forward with it, for better or worse.

It's impossible for readers to feel the emotions we did. They were strong, continued for over two years, and created extreme feelings of resentment. The subject of this piece belittled subordinates, degraded peers, and viciously insulted others not working for the company. She did it all under the veil of security in an organization which thought highly of her professionalism and leadership. Many knew, but none dared speak a word of it! Sure, it would be easy to point fingers at the company overall, but it was eventually determined they were ignorant to what was unfolding. Therefore, this is more about an individual than an organization.

The culture was drastically deteriorating, and depending on your manager, it was either going well, or not. I'd commiserate with others in different regions with gripes analogous with mine because those at our level were always looking to vent. As they say, misery loves company! It's usually the ones on the bottom who absorb the brunt of the emotional beatings, and the bruises were numerous.

I'm certain levels above experienced pressure, but their laughing and joking on team calls left us wondering if we even worked for the same company. It's sad really, because this was an industry leader, and yet little does the outside world know the real story. We felt underappreciated and of little value to the company. We thought how nice it must be just one rung up the ladder and why such a wide gap in responsibilities? If we spoke up, as on occasion, we were labeled "negative," not a team player. The company was culturally hypocritical to most of us.

I've had many managers throughout the years representing a diverse spectrum. I never once judged them on their background, religious belief, sexual preference, or ethnicity. For me, they were my superior and I went about doing my job. Each treated me, and others, respectfully, long before the changes taking place over the last decade in society.

Abruptly, I was in the unenviable position of having to report to whom I consider the absolute worst boss ever! She had a reputation of being a micromanager, but I was ignorant to what level, or the classless, vulgar way she conducted herself. Much of what I write is obviously opinionated, but one chapter in particular is 100% factual.

I shared these instances internally, and sought advice to what actions I should take. The advice provided was reporting her would not go well FOR ME. I found this extremely contradictory since the company encouraged feedback for inappropriate behavior. We were all about "integrity and respect" (what company isn't?) and yet exposing a wrong was frowned upon? The advice could have been inaccurate, but since it came from a trusted source, I took it to heart.

It's unfortunate for any company to behave this way, and issues will never be addressed if employees are suppressed. I get the whole "whistle-blowing" concept, but when the actions are as egregious as what you'll read, it ultimately brings more shame to a company to silence employees than to accept honest, candid feedback.

Subsequently, fate intervened and I fell victim to a company-wide restructuring. Upon being notified I was let go, I felt relieved with the ability to share what I'd been holding back for years. Finally, I could unload this nightmare and attempt to foster support for others in the process.

My initial thought was to write a tell-all book, yet it wasn't the message I wanted to publicize. I didn't want to come across with an axe to grind in general, because my animosity was directed toward an individual, not an entire organization. Recently, someone with far more knowledge of just how vile this individual was inquired if I had any dirt on them. Dirt would be putting it mildly. What I had would be better constituted as raw sewage!

We often say don't take work home with you, or leave your personal troubles at the door when you come to work. In the position we were placed, those "asks" were difficult to adhere to. I considered myself a hard worker and to have it end working for this person was more than I could endure. We were a small team of only six, and at least three other members—I made four—loathed her to no end! I don't believe she ever realized how despised she was, and probably is to this day!

So, in addition to telling my story, I use this as a guide for all. Be respectful of individuals you interact with, and choose your words carefully. Things you say, whether in private or not, can come back to haunt you. There's simply no need for this bigotry, and the winds of change have been blowing for some time now.

This is my story.

For Mom and Dad, whom I respect more today than ever! May they be resting peacefully!

Table of Contents

Introduction i
1 The Beginning of the End 1
2 The Micromanaging 9
3 Good Cop, Bad Cop 23
4 20 Warning Signs You Are Working
    For the Wrong Leader 29
5 Did She Really Just Say That? 43
Epilogue 59

1

The Beginning of the End

Mondays were office days and I had the pleasure of working kitty-corner from my best friend and coworker (BFCW). At the time, we were on the same team working for a manager who was very hands-off and who had only recently joined the department.

The company had many departments which to distribute products to Consumers. There were corporates stores, an on-line presence, a B2B department, National Retail Accounts and Authorized Retailers. Often times they competed with each other as much as they did other companies. It created friction, but nothing that couldn't be resolved amongst leadership.

I'd never worked in other departments, but many in our group claimed the difference was night and day. I can't speak to it personally, so I took them at their word. There was definitely pressure on them to not only produce, but report on the day's activities when the stores closed late at night, past bedtime for some. Metrics they were measured on seemed "out there" and I recall speaking to a manager in another department saying it was ridiculous! We shared some of the same metrics, but not all, so we didn't have to deal with identical issues. Again, not having worked there, I'd have no way of knowing what life was like for them. That's not to say we didn't have our own challenges.

Our group supported authorized retailers of our products, made up of larger, national players, and local, smaller ones. The front-line turnover was high, and we were constantly training, coaching, and developing new hires. It was a main focus of the position and I enjoyed that function over reporting or the administrative duties required. For the most part, we got along well, but with so many personalities involved, you were bound to encounter one or two you wouldn't see eye to eye with, mainly because they didn't work FOR US. I admit, my personality clashed with a couple of them and I share responsibility for that.

I visited a store soon after launching a particular product, and the company didn't regard them as "worthy" of carrying it, because of their low productivity. They had a great location in town, but were unable to maximize sales potential. And in the business I was in, location, and to a degree staffing, was everything! So it was perplexing they couldn't produce the results required.

As I walked into the store, I saw the owner jump from behind his computer and yell, "Get the fuck out of my store!" Needless to say, I was startled by his outburst and silently withstood the verbal lashing regarding "the product." You see, his sales were dropping because his twelve (I'm exaggerating) customers were now shopping elsewhere to get it. Soon after, we canceled our contract with him and moved on to other things. I found out later, prior to being hired, my manager at the time came close to punches with him over something else he didn't agree with. This was the only negative interaction I had worth noting!

It's not our ship!

Our group was the first, and quite possibly the only one, to have gone through a year-long program called *It's Your Ship*. It's a fascinating read about how the worst ship in the navy transformed into the best, by a captain getting the most out of his crew. If you haven't read it, I highly recommend it! Much of what he writes is making sure you have the right people in the right positions, based on desires and skill sets. Truly a must-read across all levels of management within a company!

However, many of us pondered why we were going through this, because our company didn't really behave this way. I mean, this went on for months and there came a point when we had an open discussion regarding the "elephant in the room," as someone put it. We brought attention to the trainers that this wasn't how our company was run, and asked why we were wasting our time. Others shied away from providing feedback out of fear it would get back to our senior manager, the one responsible for enrolling us. Anyway, we never got a decent answer and continued until completion. It was unfortunate because the book, and philosophy projected, is a benefit to organizations. Just wasn't ours.

I reference this because there's a line in the book that states, "Micromanaging does not work!" As a former manager leading a team, I adhered to the philosophy and always worked to ensure group success. If there was a member lagging behind, we rallied around to provide support, and always as a team. I wasn't going to allow failure—not because it might reflect negatively on me, but because I cared for them personally. This was my ship!

So, on a particular Monday, BFCW and I overheard this new manager running a team call. We couldn't believe the micromanaging going on and how thankful we were for not reporting to "Cruella." She was a retread from another department who'd never held our position. Yes, a real know-it-all who proclaimed to tell us what our job was and how we should do it. Rumor has it she stated on more than one occasion our level did absolutely nothing! Never said it to me, so I can't verify the accuracy of it, but having subsequently worked for Cruella, I could absolutely picture her mouthing something so ignorant! She obviously didn't know what we had to do!

It fascinates me how someone who'd never held a particular role could comment on that role's responsibilities. The first thing I did when managing a position I hadn't held previously was solicit feedback from subordinates on what worked and what improvements we should make. Take my advice on this one, if you didn't do the job, avoid proclaiming to know it!

By now, a couple of years had passed since that entertaining Monday, and late one afternoon, I received a call from my BFCW. She was literally hyperventilating because she was told there were changes coming and she'd now be reporting to Cruella. I thought she was going to lose it and resign on the spot, so I used all my support mechanisms to talk her off the ledge and ease her anxieties. Ultimately, she wasn't the one moving to the "dark side." It was me!

I relived that discussion over and over when times were unbearable and I knew she'd never have lasted working for Cruella. And I say this with all due respect considering she was an exceptional worker who didn't require micromanaging whatsoever. Her gain was so much my loss!

The fateful call came from my manager while we still were under the impression my BFCW was going. When he informed me, he said, "I'm not the micromanaging type she is, so I hope you're okay with it." I took it as professionally as I could, and regardless, there really wasn't much I could do. Still, I was glad my BFCW wasn't transferred and I would be the one absorbing the hit. Like I was taking one for the team!

Then it hit me…I was now on a sinking ship!

2
The Micromanaging

Imagine having previously attended a year-long program emphasizing how ineffective micromanaging was, and then suddenly find you're working for the ultimate micromanager. This was my life now.

I was older than most of my coworkers and believe this possibly contributed to my frustration. I'd been in the workforce for over forty years and at this point shouldn't have to endure such an outdated management approach. Didn't bother me my boss was female, younger, or rumored to have little education beyond high school. Rather, it was her style that irritated, and upon hearing others shared similar emotions, mine were justified. Good to know, but equal to securing a Band-Aid on a hemorrhage.

Some of what I share might sound petty or trivial, but it goes back to the impossibility of knowing what life was like unless you experienced it firsthand. There were times of disgust, bitterness, and outright disdain which we endured for years on end, and it was all because she made us do far more than the job required and what other teams in the same position had to do. This doesn't mean the other managers didn't have their own flaws in some way, but it didn't cause their teams to want to turn on them, as we did.

The tasks were unfathomable, no exaggeration, and by no means drove results! When I explained my new workload to my BFCW, she couldn't believe it! After all, we shared the same position, but not the same set of rules or workload. Our team wasted more time on activities designed to make Cruella look good in a review and less time actually being productive. God forbid you didn't have one of these nonsensical things done, because you'd inevitably receive an email or text message to complete it right away.

Another manager informed me she was pushing her agenda on them to have their teams follow suit. Their response was "We're all set, thank you!" but if that had transpired, a mutiny would have ensued. Bad enough one team had to endure it, but to have an entire region micromanaged would have sent people packing. That was her way of getting recognition, by projecting her fruitless activities on others. Little did she realize how out of touch she was, yet ironically, on a couple of occasions she did actually get her way. Knowing her, it must have pissed her off the region didn't initiate more of her childish agenda. Like I started with, it's impossible to understand the emotions fully, but here goes…

The Schedule

One of these items in particular was the schedule, filled out the beginning of each month. I wasn't against it—in fact I had to do it for other managers, but what bothered me was the number of times she reached out asking where we were going to be on a particular day. How about you just read the damn schedule you make us fill out? Seriously, it must have been dozens upon dozens of times. And seeing as we went through more fire drills than I could count, the schedule would constantly be changing anyway! That's another thing, the constant focus of chasing different metrics based on how Cruella was doing against her peers. It was a "flavor of the week" atmosphere and this I blame more on the company than her. Still, it was more wasted time, but then again, she knew our job, right?

And the color-coding! Not only did we have to fill the schedule out monthly, we had to shade the days all these different colors based on what we were doing that particular day. It was fourth-grade stuff (nothing against fourth graders) and I remember a coworker proclaiming she was trying to parent rather than manage. It was truly a joke, and we would make up our own stuff and rail about what color should this or that be! As much as she was driving us over the edge, we did our very best to humor ourselves in order to get by. But it was genuinely degrading being told you don't have enough "purple" depicted on your schedule.

At one point she wanted us to send Outlook invitations first of the month to all the owners, and then put them in the calendar. The owners didn't have time for this because not only was their schedule extremely volatile, but it was impossible for them to plan a whole month's worth of activity in advance. And why should they simply because my manager wanted them to? I suggested upon confirming a day and time, we could then send out the invite and secure it in the calendar. My peers actually agreed with me and yet it got shot down like every other good idea I brought. It was only going to be her way, and more on that in the coming chapters.

As is usually the case, life gets in the way sometimes and people need to adjust their schedules accordingly. Once, a coworker had his water heater replaced early in the morning so as to not upset his whole day. He proactively called Cruella to inform her he'd be working from home for a couple of hours while this was taking place. We had plenty of work to accomplish on the computer early in the morning anyway, so there should have been no issue.

What did she do? Directed him to put it in his timesheet as "personal time." He was livid and shared those feelings with me. Was she serious? It's not like he was the one actually installing the unit; he was upstairs working on his computer while the professionals did it. There was another instance of her telling us to put in for personal time while in the midst of a blizzard. How stupid is that? The stores are closed, the company wants us off the road and safe, and Cruella is directing us to take personal time? The other managers talked some sense into her, and she backed off from that little gem. Personal time….good one, Cruella!

Here's the hypocrisy in all this. Often we either couldn't get hold of her, or we waited hours to hear back. We felt she was screwing off and taking advantage of the fact that she really didn't have the workload we had. There were often times you'd speak with her and hear the dog barking in the background or the microwave running or dishes being washed. Others had sworn on Fridays in the summer, she'd be sitting by the pool in her backyard killing time getting some rays! Hypocrite!

When we wouldn't hear from her for a few days, we'd suddenly get the barrage. You might go a day or two without the nagging and then all of a sudden, she'd be sitting at home and start rapid-firing off emails and text messages. Before you could finish reading one, the next would arrive with a directive. *I need you to do this or that, and call all your stores and get them to increase that one thing I'm behind in!* It was a constant and not an atmosphere anybody relished. Seriously, we were living a horrible existence, and it reminded me of that show *Horrible Bosses* and wasn't there a way to showcase Cruella?

One thing the company emphasized was no overtime! The position required us to be on call when our doors were open, which included nights and weekends. There simply was too much work for us to get done in a forty-hour schedule. A coworker documented a separate timesheet of the hours he worked in a week and it was eye-opening! He did this for months and the difference between what we HAD to input and what was ACTUAL was major! Mind you, back when we were able to declare overtime, we were compensated half our wage! I always thought overtime equaled time and a half, not half time. Another sore spot for employees, but we couldn't question the legality of it all.

The Daily Forecast Sheet

In addition to the "rainbow" schedule, we had to populate a Daily Forecast Sheet based on the previous year's month, by day. We had to input the individual numbers and then populate a section broken down by product, and still another to forecast activities that month.

Fortunately, we didn't have to adolescently color-code it.

Filling it out was easy, but we had to access it on our computers every Monday, and this is where it gets monotonous. Each team member would read out their weekly results, while WE WERE ALL LOOKING AT THE SAME SHEET! Listen, if I wanted to know what Bobby or Janie was doing each week, I'd simply access it and take note. It wasn't necessary for everyone to do a read-out individually when we were all viewing it. Another time-wasted activity. No doubt, everyone knew where they were during the month and what was needed to finish positively. In other words, we were focused!

This, along with the schedule, was not being pushed onto other teams by their managers. They had their own deal, but nothing compared to what we endured. And like I said, Cruella wasn't even looking at the spreadsheets she was making us populate.

Weekly Team Calls

You remember in Chapter One my BFCW and I rolling our eyes listening to Cruella run her team calls while we worked for someone else? Well, I was the lucky one experiencing the gastrointestinal pain now. Toward the end, I was pounding omeprazole like gummy bears!

Other than the proverbial Daily Forecast Sheet read-out by team member, there was the nails-on-a-chalkboard lecture to digest as well! Inevitably, we would come out of these calls with yet another item on our already full plate. Between what we had to do FOR HER and what our ACTUAL JOB WAS, the tasks were beginning to take their toll. Yet, ironically, she proclaimed working to lessen our load. You know, because she knew what we had to do! Really, you know because you've done our job? Let's not even go there again!

Most had lost all respect for her. I can't speak for the entire team, but I know factually more than half did. The way she behaved, treated us, and the micromanaging was overbearing, unnecessary, and unproductive. My BFCW would've caved early on! Post the dreaded read-outs, she would talk on endlessly about absolutely nothing, with little ever gained. No doubt you've experienced this and know how excruciating it can be week in and week out. Nobody wants to hear someone babble for an hour when nothing good comes of it. She was obviously justifying her existence within the company by filling time! There wasn't a single instance when I hung up from this call having learned something or discovered another way to increase productivity. Proclaiming her as ineffective is an understatement!

Group Messages

At all hours of the day, she'd send *War and Peace* length messages to the group. Another annoying undertaking because we knew she was sitting at home searching for something to do, so why not start riding the team? That was a majority of the problem in hindsight, nothing to do really and all day to do it! Not only was she creating work for herself, it was ultimately more work for us!

Anyway, we'd scroll down the message searching for something worthwhile in it and eventually come to the end where she asks us to confirm we received it. We'd be out in the field actually doing our job and might not see it for a bit, and she'd call again if we hadn't already responded. It got so annoying, the team would simply put in short replies like "Yup," "Got it," "Sure," and things like that. If we didn't reply, she'd ask "are you still with us?" with "lol" behind it. It was her way of letting us know she was still waiting. What was taking us so long to respond? Um, we're working, Cruella!

Of course every one of these messages had significant typos, making them arduous to read and borderline comical. It was hieroglyphics and would lead to a smaller, separate set of messages amongst a select group, if you know what I mean. The typos were always the phone's fault.

Throughout her time on the team, it was a common occurrence for her to have issues with her phone, tablet, and laptop. The best was when she would tell you this and then ask someone to do something for her because her devices weren't working properly. Any room for this on your plate? Sure, let me get right on that for you, Cruella!

I often thought about hitting the lottery (who doesn't?) and "ghosting" her. Not answering her emails, calls, or group messages. Simply disappearing into the night knowing it would drive her insane and leave her to answer for it. Others shared the sentiments and were awaiting the opportunity!

3

Good Cop, Bad Cop

My industry involved creating solid relationships with outside partners. As referenced in the first chapter, I had, for the most part, good working relationships and a couple that went south. It happens.

I would visit these folks every other week, if not more, so they knew what to expect when I walked in the door, as did I. I was never one to beat down on them, and always worked hard to soften the message from above. That's not to say we didn't have tough conversations at times, but I always let them know we were in this together and it wasn't a one-way street!

It was our responsibility to visit stores daily, but on occasion, those at Cruella's level would also engage in this activity. Cruella might visit doors of mine maybe once a year. The closer they were to her residence, the more she might frequent them, and unfortunately for me, MY stores were closest to her home. She would saunter in them being as polite and phony as she could be, putting on a real charade. A favorite of hers was to police the locations for cleanliness, and ultimately either vacuum or dust and play the role of happy homemaker. I'd always hear about it after the fact how sloppy and lazy the store was, but she never once brought it up directly to them.

Some thought she was okay, and others saw right through it. In the end, they were asking me how they could get her off of their account and secure another, more productive manager. They began to learn just how two-faced she was, and it grated on them as much as it did us. Others simply let what she had to say go in one ear and out the other, not even bothering to reference the directive she was projecting.

On one specific occasion, she called to have me deliver a message to a store that showed football games on their big screen Sundays in the fall. She wanted them to run a company loop showcasing our products and services, and stop with the games. They had other screens showing the loop, so to have one showing a sporting event was okay by me. Like it was yesterday, I called the owner to relay this message and his response was "She can go fuck herself!" Okay then, I'll let you be the one to pass that tidbit along. You see, the games were bringing people into his store, which was in a mall, and he was getting ancillary business from it. People are passionate about their home team in this region of the country, and time was set aside when they were playing! According to him, his store was the only one in the mall showing the games, so I could see his point.

When Cruella finally had the chat with him, via text, she told him to simply have the channel (on the TV) changed and finished it with a "lolololol."

What? Is that how you want to play this? It was like that scene in *Braveheart* where William Wallace says to Robert the Bruce, "If you would just LEAD, people would follow you! I would follow you!" Instead, it was more Longshanks…making her team look like jerks and her coming off like a charm! She was weak when it came to this, and always massaged their egos in order to have them play nice in the sand. We were the bad guys!

This was the same store she referenced in a call complaining the employees were a "bunch of lazy pricks." (More on the phone calls coming up.) I'm giving you one example, but there are many more. Like the time she referred to one group of women as "fucking dumpy" because they looked as though "they hadn't washed their hair in a fucking month." I didn't get the directive, but imagine me having to tell the women in the store to wash their hair because my manager thought they looked dumpy. Honestly, you can't make this up!

The classic "Wolf and Red Riding Hood" gig when it came to tough conversations. Even when I had serious concerns regarding their business practices and brought them forward, she simply shrugged them off because they were helping her numbers, albeit false ones.

I golfed once with a senior manager at a fundraising event and although not working for him directly, he knew it was early in my career there. He shared some great advice, and as he was a veteran of the company in a position of leadership, I listened intently. He said, *"No matter how good you are, it will never be good enough."* You see, this was the culture and now, more than ever, I realized just how accurate that statement was!

4

20 Warning Signs You Are Working For the Wrong Leader

A peer sent out a link to a column written about the 20 Warning Signs You Are Working For the Wrong Leader, in direct reference to Cruella. Once my day was done, I accessed it and starting going down the list one by one. To my amazement, the article, written by Glenn Llopis for *Forbes*, was describing Cruella precisely, as if the author had done a piece specifically on her! I include it here because the resemblance was uncanny, and a lesson for all managers to take note of.

This was her…

1. Always Negative

Leaders that see the glass half empty lack optimism and hope. They deflate your excitement and discourage your passionate pursuits of endless possibilities. Oftentimes negative leaders grow envious of your capabilities that they are unable to perform themselves.

2. Don't Encourage

Leaders who are not lifting and guiding you to reach your full potential are not doing their job. Their world is centered upon their needs, not yours. Many times they don't encourage you because they are threatened and see you as standing in the way of their glory.

When a leader constantly pulls you down, you begin to feel as if you don't really matter and that your sole responsibility is to follow and do what you are told. This type of leader makes it difficult for you to grow and prosper.

3. Are Not Grateful

Leaders that don't appreciate or acknowledge your hard work and contributions also set a negative tone in the organization. It surprises me just how many leaders don't take the time to say "thank you" or send a simple follow-up email of gratitude. Though they expect you to do your job, they don't have to take you for granted.

Being grateful is an easy way to give employees more recognition and respect. Never take employees for granted. If you do, don't expect their loyalty and trust – let alone their willingness to keep meeting your performance expectations.

4. High Maintenance

When a leader's expectations begin to expose their own weaknesses, you have been dealt a high-maintenance individual. High-maintenance leaders demand too much because they don't understand the job well enough to effectively delegate.

High-maintenance leaders become another full-time job for employees, and this gets in the way of delivering on their own responsibilities—let alone the additional ones assumed for the leader incapable of effectively leading his or her team. (Sounds exhausting, don't it.)

5. Too Controlling

Leaders that want to control everything are those that don't empower you to think freely. When leaders are too controlling this is a sign that they do not trust their employees enough to manage the tasks at hand.

Controlling leaders stifle employee growth, development and maturity—and by extension that of the organization.

6. Manipulative

Leaders that lift you and inspire hope—only to then leech from you (to bring you back down) are the most manipulative and untrustworthy of leaders. Every leader has an agenda and if it requires manipulative tactics to propel the organization and/or their department forward, there is eventually going to be high employee turnover.

It's difficult to co-exist in a workplace environment that is fueled by leaders that manipulate, rather than authentically stimulate growth and opportunities for their employees. Manipulation is a short-term approach that is not sustainable.

7. Lack Self-Trust

When leaders lack self-trust, how can they aid their employees' advancement when they don't have the confidence to advance their own? When leaders lack self-trust they begin to steal the ideas of others to manage their own reputation. This is why many leaders quickly become followers when the going gets tough. This is not an attractive proposition for employees that are in search of a leader that they can learn from and that can teach them new ways of doing things.

8. Hide From Accountability

For some leaders, paying it forward means letting others deal with the problems they should have solved themselves. Accountability is the number one thing that great managers learn to master. Once you become a leader, it should become second nature as your influence grows.

Leaders that push down accountability to wipe their hands clean of any wrongdoing immediately lose respect from their employees. Leaders that hide when you need them most are the ones that won't help you solve your problems. Employees get discouraged when leaders don't act in their best interests.

9. Disorganized

A disorganized leader is one that lacks organized thinking and thus has a greater tendency to put their employees in a position of risk. When leaders are disorganized it creates disruption and a malfunctioning part of the business.

Employees expect their leaders to be organized as it is a reflection of their style and approach and commitment to serving others.

10. Know It All

Some leaders want to believe they have all the answers and expect others to always do things their way. Leaders that profess to "know it all" are usually the ones that lack any real creativity or original thought. These are the types of leaders that read books only to steal the ideas of others to solve problems and position the intelligence as their own.

When leaders believe they have all of the answers, they make it difficult for their employees to share their own. Self-centeredness is a highly unattractive quality. It's never fun to be led by someone whose ego stands in the way of your success.

11. No Vision for the Future

It's difficult to respect a leader that doesn't know where they want to take the organization and how to develop the right succession plans for their employees. People that are uncertain about the future lack the required entrepreneurial attitude to create a roadmap that keeps renewing and refreshing the organization and its people.

When leaders are unable to "connect the dots" of opportunity—their employees begin to disconnect quickly.

12. Lack Strong Decision-Making Skills

When leaders lack the ability to make decisions, this leaves a bad taste in the mouths of employees. It's difficult to get excited about a leader that lacks the instincts and know-how to go about making the right decisions. Many times leaders begin to depend upon others too much or they get into a decision-making rut. Others realize they have no one to turn to for help when the time comes to be accountable for the decisions that need to be made.

Employees want decisive, forward-thinking leaders that take pride in being on-point with their decisions so as to minimize any potential problems that might come the organization's way.

13. Incompetent

Just because you are in a leadership role doesn't guarantee that you are the most knowledgeable person in the room. When you lack the required depth, substance, and competence to be an effective leader, it makes it difficult to build a reputation to be proud of—or that your employees can share with clients, vendors, strategic partners, etc.

14. Micromanages

When your judgment is constantly second-guessed and when you feel as if every move you make is being monitored or questioned by your leader, it's impossible to get excited about your work. Leaders that micromanage are those that have trouble letting go of their own self-doubt and insecurities about themselves and/or the people they lead.

Micromanagement is extremely annoying for employees that are looking to get discovered at work; instead they feel the angst of being under constant surveillance.

15. Poor Listeners

Leaders that don't take the time to listen to what their employees are saying are the ones that continue to miss the opportunities that lie right in front of them. Most problems are solved and opportunities previously unseen are discovered through listening. Leaders may not always realize it, but their employees know when they are not listening to them.

Poor listeners are inconsistent leaders. They turn off their employees who are not being heard and make them feel as if their voices don't matter.

16. Lack Attention to Detail

Great leaders see what others don't, do what others won't, and keep pushing when prudence says quit. Attention to detail is what enables us to see what lies around, beneath and beyond the obvious—and keeps everyone on their toes.

When leaders lack attention to detail it gives people pause about what their leaders may not be seeing about employee growth and career development requirements.

17. Don't Practice What They Preach

Leaders that don't practice what they preach are not following their own rules. This makes it difficult to value what your leader expects from you if they don't play by the same game plan.

When leaders say one thing and do another, they lack the authenticity that is required to be a trustworthy leader.

18. Lack Consistency

Leaders that lack consistency in their approach, style, and how they run their business are difficult to rely upon.

Consistency is an undervalued leadership trait that matters most to employees and that leaders must develop in their quest to earn respect and trust. Employees expect their leaders to have the discipline, structure, and mindfulness to deliver great and consistent leadership in everything they do and how they do it.

19. Dishonest

Dishonesty comes packaged in all shapes and sizes and when leaders are dishonest with their employees, it is challenging to get behind them or believe anything they say.

These types of leaders often have hidden agendas and come across as too political at best, devious and inauthentic at worst. Dishonesty is the surest and fastest way to lose trust from employees, and once lost it may never be regained.

20. Identity Crisis

Leaders that are challenged by points 1 – 19 are the ones that have a leadership identity crisis. When leaders can't define their identity as a leader, it makes it difficult for them to live what they stand for—and a challenge for their employees and colleagues to experience the real person that they are. As a result, they battle the gulf between assimilation and authenticity trying to figure out where they fit at work and how they should be leading others.

When leaders don't know their own identity, they get lost in the rush of business necessity. This is when they—often unknowingly—begin to show many of the 20 warning signs discussed here. This makes it difficult for them to lead in ways that come most naturally to them.

But it's even more difficult to work for such a leader—one that isn't genuine and can't be trusted to reveal their employees' strengths and opportunities for advancement.

5

Did She Really Just Say That?

Every night at 7:30, I make myself available to watch *Jeopardy*. It's a habit, and depending on the category, I fare pretty well. I share it with you because I have a recurring dream involving both Jeopardy and Cruella.

In the dream, I've had a good run and make it to Final Jeopardy with the money lead! Alex proceeds to announce the category – "Worst Boss Ever." "Contestants, make your wages, and we'll be right back with the clue after these messages from our sponsor." I can feel my palms sweat and it's not about winning the money; it's being called Jeopardy Champion! Am I the only one having this dream? Commercial break is over and it's time to hear the clue and reveal our answers.

Alex: "Contestents, here's the clue. Who is considered to be the Worst Boss Ever? Please write down your answers."

Alex: "Julie, you go first. So what is your response?"

Julie: "Who is Bernie Madoff."

Alex: "That's incorrect, and how much will it cost you? Oh, all you have, so you're down to $0. George, you're up next and who did you choose?"

George: "Who is Harvey Weinstein."

Alex: "Nope, sorry, that's also incorrect, and how much did you wager? All of it as well, so you're down to $0, tied with Julie at the moment."

Alex: "Christopher, your game to win or lose. Let's see your response. 'Who is Cruella,' and that is correct! Cruella is obviously the worst boss ever and how much did you wager? All! Christopher, you're our new Jeopardy Champion! See you all back here tomorrow night, folks!"

Great dream!

The company had a program just for women, designed to foster career opportunities and help develop select young females into leaders. I personally loved the concept and hoped more companies were conducting these programs. Many close friends were awarded the chance to attend, and feedback was extremely positive!

Cruella was chosen as "mentor" for this program, and having worked almost two years now for her, I questioned the appointment. I have plenty of reasons for that opinion, and in the following pages I share why. Regardless, she was the "golden girl" in someone's eye, and in hindsight, that person is either a succinctly bad judge of character or doesn't know the real Cruella! Over phone calls made to me by her, or things she said while together, it's appalling and true!

While developing this chapter, I wanted to recall every single inappropriate thing. She had something to say about everyone, a gossipy person, and in her heart felt it "cool" to be vulgar. She was unpolished and in this particular instance, you can take the girl out of the city, but you can't take the city out of the girl! I'm listing them in order of unprofessionalism and vulgarity. We'll start out slow and move on to the unfathomable!

What you're about to read is the truth, the whole truth, and nothing but the truth. So help me, God!

Phone call # 1

When a coworker was on vacation or out on leave, we had to cover for them. We all took turns because it was something we had to do, and given it doubled our workload, we tried to spread it around.

I was covering for a peer who was doing a river cruise in Eastern Europe with a stop in Russia. I forgot how long she was going to be out for, but I remember it being longer than the usual week. This peer had been with the company for many years and was actually close to retiring. I believe in the end it was Cruella who prompted the early exit simply because she couldn't deal with the culture being laid upon us.

Cruella disliked this person and would find ways to annoy the ever-loving daylights out of her. I'm surprised she lasted as long as she did under these conditions, and like some of us, she'd reach out and vent her frustrations. This is a woman who'd give you her kidney if you were a match and needed it. Everyone had positive things to say about her, and she'd bake cookies and treats for her stores during occasions and even wrap them up uniquely as if from a high-end specialty store! It was a gift she had, especially around the holidays!

So I called Cruella to see when this person was coming back, and it was at that moment I got a real taste of her animosity toward her. She said, "Hopefully never!"

"What?" I said.

"I hope the Russians throw her overboard and she never comes back!"

Again, this woman had been with the company for many years, was well respected, and would give you the shirt off her back! This infamous comment later became known as the "Throw Momma from the Train" remark to a select few I shared it with.

Unfortunately, it was a sign of things to come, and the more she trusted me, the more vulgar it became. And that trust increased my discomfort level from simply shaking my head, to reaching out internally for advice. In hindsight, what I really needed was a therapist, some good meds, and a comfy couch.

Phone call # 2

Cruella was visiting stores and happened upon one of mine. She called to say the store was sloppy and the girl never got up from behind the counter to greet her. I hated her visiting my stores unannounced and unchaperoned, as did others, because if they looked hard enough, they could always find something wrong! Either the wrong poster was up, or a light was out and the floor was dirty. It wasn't easy keeping up, and because they didn't work directly for us, it made it that much more challenging.

More than one woman worked there, so I asked which one. "The fat chick" was her response. I was just shaking my head, thinking the poor kid, adults really, having to deal with her two-faced abuse, because I know for a fact she was as polite as could be while there.

I knew who she meant and if Cruella realized how nice a person she was, the insult might have been omitted. This is probably not as violent an outburst as others you'll read, but nonetheless, can you imagine? My own daughter experienced this in school and was mercilessly ridiculed for being overweight. Now this supposedly mature adult was acting like one of those bullies. Cruella had her own young children, and I thought how devastated she would be if it happened to them! Sad and disheartening at the same time!

Phone call # 3

Shortly after I joined the team, I received a call from Cruella in a tizzy over a coworker. This was a person highly respected and extremely adept at reporting, and more precisely, Excel. He would spend more time than others in the office, and I swear it bothered the heck out of her! I was the opposite, logging in to my computer at 6:30 a.m. and visiting stores upon opening.

He got under her skin, stood up to her, and never backed down. He was also soft-spoken, kept to his business, and was a great resource for others at our level, especially when it came to reporting! If we were having trouble, we would always reach out to him for advice. The entire region admired him!

Taking the call, the first words I heard out of her foul mouth were "He's a fucking pussy!" Hold on, you're calling me to claim my peer was what? I found this extremely unsettling and although I let it go, I realized I was dealing with a manager type I had never dealt with before. She obviously trusted I wouldn't say anything because the hits just kept on coming!

I felt horrible not informing him, but was concerned I'd actually hurt his feelings and do more harm than good. Given her nature, I'm sure she said similar things about me to others or to others about others. It was egregious, but there was more to come!

Ride-Along

Shortly after Cruella was chosen as that aforementioned mentor, we did a ride-along to one of my stores. Upon conclusion of the visit, she said we had to swing over to another store for a bit. This wasn't one of mine, so I asked, "Why?" She said she had to "go meet this fucking mentoring bitch!" Oh my god! I mean, you can't fathom my abhorrence and to be honest, as creative and imaginative as I think I am, I'd fall way short on this one!

This "mentoring bitch" she's referring to was one of the chosen few to go through this program. It was an honor, and Cruella was showing her true colors (not on the schedule) by simply having to meet the poor kid. It came across like a major inconvenience which she didn't have time for. I confess, this was definitely the time I should have said something, and if I hadn't previously been told it wouldn't end well for me, I would have. I fought with myself over this predicament and wished she never confided in me this way.

During subsequent ride-alongs, she'd talk smack about how this woman was a slut because she was married and "banging" two guys in the office, or how this one was trashy because she was "fucking a guy" from work in her house, while her husband was out. I mean, what type of person actually goes around saying these things about their peers, to a subordinate?

It was so matter-of-fact and callous. How serious was she taking this mentoring gig anyway? It was as if she could say anything she wanted, being "the golden girl," an "untouchable."

Phone call # 4

Keep in mind, it's 2018 and there's a lot going on in the country! You have the "Me Too" movement, LGBTQ marches, and a harkening back to the civil rights protests in cities and towns. It was a time to embrace the sensitivities, and I was working for the most vulgar, insensitive person I'd ever known. If there was ever a time to watch what you said, it was now!

Once again, Cruella sauntered into a store while on the road. It had been mine when they originally opened, but a peer was now responsible. Anyway, she couldn't wait to ring me on her ride back to proclaim whom she'd met.

"I just met so-and-so!"

My response was "Oh really? I love her!"

"Yes, I just met her and had no idea she was a bull dyke!"

LORD HAVE MERCY! I literally choked on my coffee and pulled into a parking lot! The numbness left me denying I actually heard this foul, derogatory term! Everyone I know, including myself, has a gay family member, friend, or coworker, and categorizing them this way was beyond reproach! You were chosen as a "mentor"? Wait, maybe that's not what she said and I simply heard the wrong thing! When I shared this with a couple of people, not on our team, they confessed to also having heard her use this term, as if it were a favorite of hers.

I had the utmost respect and admiration for this person being belittled! The fact she was lesbian never entered my mind during our interactions, and I was once again left flabbergasted by the conduct of my immediate supervisor! It was an uneasy feeling and I seriously entertained the thought of throwing caution to the wind. But would spilling the beans cost me my job, my income, my 401(k), my medical insurance, my home? My head was on spin cycle and it was overwhelming!

Phone call # 5

Cruella called me returning from a review one afternoon and I inquired how it went. Little did I know what that innocent question would result in. She proceeded to unload on another manager, at her level, from a different market.

This woman had always been mistreated by a larger group of managers closer to my area. It was like *Mean Girls*, whereby one group bullies someone who isn't in their clique. She and Cruella were oil and water. They had already confronted each other at offsite meetings, and this was Cruella's opportunity to lash out and get revenge!

"So-and-so is a C**T!" The dreaded "C" word! She actually spelled it out and didn't say the word. Floored, I responded, "Excuse me?"

She said, "You heard me and let me tell you why. She claims to visit each of her stores eight times a quarter, so that's over five hundred, and she's full of shit! Can you believe it?"

Um, what I can't believe actually is your description of a peer! What say we start with that? My closest friends will tell you how much I despise this word. To me, it's the most vulgar word in the English language, and not only have I never used it, I don't enjoy watching movies with the term in it. Yikes!

How do you even begin to address this with your boss? My discomfort level was maxed out now and I was clueless how to address it. In all my years of employment, never had I been in this position! It was foreign to me, so I reached out to another manager I was close with to share this verbal assault. It was then I was told I'd be better off keeping my mouth shut! Bringing this up to HR would not work out well for me because she had seen it happen previously. I was so appalled I had to stop what I was doing and take a deep breath!

I couldn't help but think if the roles were reversed, I'd be terminated in a heartbeat! Was it because I was a man and it was okay if a woman said it about another woman? I was sincerely dumbfounded, and handcuffed with the ability to speak up!

In hindsight, it might have been okay to look the other way if it happened maybe once or twice. But the behavior continued over a two-year span, and the more it went on, the more unbelievable it became. A few of my coworkers' resentment equaled mine, and like me, they wished someone would take the lead and come forward. However, they knew if they did, they'd be black-listed as I would have been too. It was 1950s McCarthyism we were living, and we kept silent more out of fear than to protect her.

I recall another occasion whereby Cruella rang up a franchise director to complain about a door he oversaw. Throughout the call, she went on about what she perceived were multiple infractions and their lack of ability to change and adhere to her ways. When the call ended, the franchise director claimed that halfway through, he stopped counting how many F-bombs she let fly. This was how she behaved when people weren't around and she felt it okay to literally tear into others in a secondhand fashion rather than to their face.

Somehow, the micromanaging seemed much more insignificant and palatable now. Being subjected to this behavior by a person considered a leader was justifiably more than one could bear.

Epilogue

I can't lie. I regret not exposing this fraud, and I blame myself. I should have summoned the strength to drop-a-dime, but I had so much at stake, I kept silent until now. I'm ashamed of it because I know she's out there still behaving this way.

Reliving all this on paper rekindled bitter emotions. Documenting it was one thing; living it was another. There were other instances during my tenure, but none reached the pinnacle these did. Ironically, she was comfortable enough to divulge her vile emotions, and yet I can't help but wonder what she might have said about me.

I guess ultimately I needed to write as a healing process. It was arguably my worst two-plus years of employment, and although others have experienced a dislike for their immediate superior, I'm pretty sure I have a leg up. Tragic really, because we're all striving to survive, earn a decent living, and possibly make a life better for ourselves than maybe our parents had. Either way, I have a deep sympathy for anyone enduring an environment such as we did.

She had the flawed ability to just speak what came to mind. Even as kids we're told that if you don't have anything nice to say about someone, don't say anything. Looking back, you'd think if she felt this way, maybe she'd save it to share over a barbeque with lifelong friends or people within her inner circle. You know those times when you've definitely had one too many! Everything was so nonchalant that it cut to the core of her character and the horrible person she truly is.

I intentionally titled this *My Worst Boss Ever* instead of *The Worst Boss Ever*, solely because it was mine and others might be able to rival it! Regardless, I challenge anyone to top it, and if they can, that's one I'm signing up to read! Although none of her comments were directed at me, I felt an obligation to expose the fact there's people like this still out there, and if the book can change the behavior of just one individual, then I will have succeeded.

Another issue I could have elaborated on was feeling "sequestered." Employees throughout the entire organization were afraid to expose wrongdoings, and that's a travesty. Integrity and respect—if you see or hear something, you have a responsibility to report it! But be careful, because you'll be black-listed for the remainder of your time with us! True hypocrisy on how reporting deplorable behavior was a double-edged sword for us.

This was a major corporation, the leader in their respective industry, and unless someone is willing to write me a check (please?) to disclose who Cruella is, I'm keeping it close to the vest. Of course, I'd be the one chastised if she's named, but if she really wanted to point fingers, I'd recommend to her a mirror! The thought of possibly being called out for not keeping MY mouth shut is ludicrous, ironic, and borderline comical! Inevitably, she'll say the wrong thing to the wrong person at the wrong time, and justice will prevail. She can't help herself.

Prior to publishing, I solicited opinions from others who knew this person, and the anecdotes they provided would fill yet another book. Theirs not only involved Cruella, but other managers they interacted with throughout their employment. I didn't include them here because they weren't MY experiences, but it gave me an idea to write a "Part 2" to this piece using their individual experiences. Hearing what they had to say would make a good read, and I was surprised at how willing they were to share their stories and how many there were! One coworker in particular stated this could have been a story about her manager, if you omitted the vulgarity. But again, this was my own personal trauma and

I'll work on theirs once this undertaking is behind me. Stay tuned!

Feedback from a few still with the company claimed Cruella had gone eerily silent upon my departure. It was said she knew I had something on her and was concerned I would go public with it. The thought of her losing sleep over it more than sufficed, and I waited weeks before writing to regain my thoughts and control my sheer spite. Once I accomplished that, the foundation was formed and the words flowed. I painstakingly went over every detail to ensure accuracy and garner readers' attention prior to submission.

I grew up middleclass, with hardworking parents. My father worked two full-time jobs while my mom stayed at home. That's how it was in those days, and we managed without all the benefits younger generations might enjoy today. One thing my parents did though was ensure we respected all regardless of where they came from or what they looked like. I carry that with me, and although no angel myself, I treat others the way I would like to be treated. At times, we've made progress and at others, like the last two years, I realize there's room to grow. Seems, as a society, we take two steps forward and one step back, but in the end, it's moving in the right direction that counts. Well, hopefully!

For those having read this book, I hope you garner another level of respect for individuals and personnel working for you or not. It's a message to embrace a more positive culture, and eradicate bigotry and discrimination. We're all different, and that alone provides an opportunity to learn and develop for the greater good. When I started my career in the '70s, there was still a lot of this going on in the world, but as my career progressed, so too did the climate throughout the country. This experience undid years of that and brought me back to that vicious timeline. One bad apple can spoil the entire barrel, or in this case, one bad manager poisoned half her team.

I hope you enjoyed the piece and gained an added appreciation for your surroundings. Life is short, so live it respectfully and as dignified as can be!

Thank you!

www.ingramcontent.com/pod-product-compliance
Lightning Source LLC
Chambersburg PA
CBHW031539210526
45464CB00003B/1073

1 di-dah-dah-dah-dah   6 dah-di-di-di-dit

2 di-di-dah-dah-dah   7 dah-dah-di-di-dit

3 di-di-di-dah-dah   8 dah-dah-dah-di-dit

4 di-di-di-di-dah   9 dih-dah-dah-dah-dit

5 di-di-di-di-dit   10 dah-dah-dah-dah-dah

Period (AAA)   di-dah-di-dah-di-dah

Question mark (IMI)   di-di-dah-dah-di-dit

Comma (MIM)   dah-dah-di-di-dah-dah

INDEX

9

9J2BO 32
9V1VV 93

A

AA3B 64
AC5K 78
AD5A 77

C

Chapter & Cover Pictures 99
classes **2, 6, 70**
code requirement **2**

D

DJ5CW **9, 13, 35, 68**

E

East Goodwin Lightship 92

F

Farnsworth **5**
filters **51**

G

G3RWF 55
G3SXW 55
G3WZD 77
G4FON 11
G6PZ 75

I

IKØIXI 47
Intl. Morse Code Alphabet **102**

J

Jean Shepherd 96

Jeremiah Denton 90

K

K1JD 77
K2ORS 96
K2TA 16
K4OSO 69
K4RLC 86
K5ALU **28, 71, 72, 74**
K5BCQ 48
K6CTW 95
K6DR 89
K7JA 95
KA4BVL 80
KBØZE 92
keys. **3, 32, 35, 36, 38, 42, 46, 47, 48, 67**
KFS 94
KM4AHP 46
Koch **5, 6, 7, 9, 11**
KØRU 71
KT5X 77
KY8D 14

L

Long Island CW Club.. **5, 7, 45, 70, 82**

N

N1FN **34, 38, 39, 43**
N3CW 48
N6XI 76
N9RV **45, 61**
New Concord 93
NJ3K 72
NØUF 48

O

ON4UN 55
ON4WW 55

P

P43JB 46
PA3EGH 48
Pro-signs 26

Q

Q-signals 27
QSK 28, 49, 50, 56

R

Relief Ship 58 93
Reverse Beacon Network 52
RST 20, 29

S

S53R 80
Samuel Morse 91
SO2R 63
SOS 93
Steve Harper 87

Straight Key Century Club 45, 67
SKCC 14
Supertanker Eriskay 93

T

The Tonight Show 95

V

VK6GX 73

W

W0FN 5
W1MP 79
W1TP 48
W2AEW 15
W6RGG 55
WA7PGR 14
WB6BEE 43, 44
WB5IW 15, 43
WD6T 83
WJ1B 48
WØVTT 72

Y

YO8SNS 99

www.ingramcontent.com/pod-product-compliance
Lightning Source LLC
Chambersburg PA
CBHW071038240526
45469CB00006BD/2245